1

THE PROPHETIC VISION

A PEAK EXPERIENCE

BY

LORNE D. GLOWICKI

THE PROPHETIC VISION

A PEAK EXPERIENCE

BY

LORNE D. GLOWICKI

CONTENTS

DEDICATED TO

The Foxes That Will Have Dens

And

The Birds That Will Have Nests

ABOUT THE BOOK

A CANADIAN APPEAL

This is a multipurpose work, primarily designed to alleviate the sufferings of Migrants and Refugees, including our First Nations, Métis and Inuit survivors of residential schools, and also many Ukrainians recently displaced by the brutal ravages of war. In Canada, our hearts and doors have been opened wide to assist in meeting the vast humanitarian needs of millions of people from around the world. This forms the basis of who we are.

Migrants and Refugees and others, combined with the dauntless spirit of **the Indigenous people,** represent the very nature of Canada. Together, our diverse cultures support our towns, villages, reserves, farmlands and urban centres, and has made our country a great and strong multicultural nation that all of us can be truly proud of.

Manitoba is the Keystone province of Canada, and of special historical significance: On October 3rd, 2023, the overwhelming majority of citizens elected an Indigenous leader as Manitoba's 1st First-Nations Premier of a Canadian province!

Winnipeg is the capital of Manitoba, and the city closes to the centre of Canada, and is also known as **the city of "Folklorama—The Festival of The Nations"** that hosts the largest and longest running multicultural event of its kind in the entire world!

"THE PROPHETIC VISION, A Peak Experience" is steeped in multiculturalism, but this particular edition is a new revision that is intended for an extra special purpose. **This book may be seen as Canada's bid to "elect" a Canadian Cardinal as the successor to one of the most effective leaders championing this humanitarian cause, Pope Francis.**

This country, along with the Vatican and a number of Cardinals and other religious institutions are fairly duty-bound to **support the Indigenous people** of Canada, severely maligned by the residential school system, by electing **a Canadian Cardinal as the next Pope.** All forms of suffering can continue to be healed more effectively when the "Highest Administrator" of *Justice and Reconciliation* is ultimately in charge.

Thankfully, **His Holiness, Pope Francis**, along with many devout others, has worked faithfully to relieve suffering, and to address the gravest challenges of ***catastrophic climate change*** facing us locally and throughout the entire world! Long may his efforts live on to fulfill the saving will of a God, the one and only one, who has no hands but ours. So, please ***join this humanitarian cause and kindly share this book*** so that all of us, as well, may continue to live on!

Appeal To All Cardinals

And for this book also to live on, it humbly makes ***a plea to all the Cardinals of the world,*** particularly those in the United States, that on that fateful day, their prayers may elect a Canadian Cardinal as **the first Pope ever** to come from the continent of North America to the glory and praise of a truly Global God!

ABOUT THE AUTHOR

Lorne Glowicki is a seasoned writer with a wealth of experience, both street-wise and life-wise. He is a former police officer, police reporter and a protective services officer, all of which has provided a fertile background for his writings.

Throughout his varied life experience, Lorne has kept his notebook close to his heart. He has filed away volumes of real-life stories, told with depth, sensitivity and his unique point of view.

His spirituality is informed by various religions and Christian denominations. This includes the Ukrainian Catholic, the United Church, the Anglican, Lutheran and Pentecostal Churches, and primarily by the Roman Catholic Church that this challenging work focuses on.

After his career in law enforcement, he formed Pyramid Agencies, an advertising specialties company. Later he invested in Applied Cybernetics Ltd., and became the Vice-President of Sales and Marketing.

After selling his business interests, he continued to work for several years as a District Deputy for a prominent international fraternal insurance agency.

Lorne resides in Winnipeg, Manitoba and lived his early childhood in the present area of the Parish of Saint Kateri Tekakwitha, and was born on the same date as her canonization, October 21st, albeit, four centuries later.

He continues to live in the North End, in another part of the city that also formed his well-earned wisdom, strong character and resilient spirit.

Kateri TekaKwitha, Patron Saint of Ecology

(Credit: Kateri Centre of Chicago)

Wab Kinew of Manitoba,

the first Canadian Province to elect

a First Nations Premier!

(Credit Mike Deal/Winnipeg Free Press}

A Magnanimous First Nations Premier
of a Canadian Province!

Wab Kinew, stepped aside, graciously assenting
to Louis Riel as the Honourary First Premier of
Manitoba, acknowledging his true place as the
founder of Manitoba, and a founding father of
the Confederation of Canada.

Inuit Tapiriit Kanatami president

Natan Obed and Pope Francis

(Credit Adam Scott/Prime Minister's Office)

The Inuit actively share the common goal with the First Nations and Métis communities in uniting all Indigenous people for the betterment of Canada.

David Chartrand

and Manitoba Métis Federation

blessed by Pope Francis at the Vatican

(Credit: CNS photo/Paul Haring)

As my book cover describes: Buried under the weight of the past, a message for the future stayed dormant for over 50 years. It remained concealed until the time prescribed for **THE PROPHETIC VISION** to be revealed.

It arose from the author's own personal and potent **PEAK EXPERIENCE**. Destined for the light, it has been released from the darkness to meet the great need of our present day. The message cries out to the nations to rescue the migrants and refugees of the world and aid in overcoming the crisis by participating in this endeavour that calls for engaging in a meaningful, international humanitarian development.

PART ONE of the book features THE PEAK EXPERIENCE leading to *PART TWO* that describes THE PROPHETIC VISION, and involves **His Holiness, Pope Francis** and the Migrants & Refugee Section of the Vatican. *PART THREE* addresses the worldwide setback imposed by the Covid-19 Pandemic that crucially hindered the development of this humanitarian cause, but also provides a way forward that may assure the ultimate success of this project by actively engaging and compassionately appealing to the **College of Cardinals**.

PART ONE

THE PEAK EXPERIENCE

The Prophetic Vision was born from a "Peak Experience". The renowned psychologist, Abraham Maslow, who developed a theory of The Hierarchy of Needs, initially coined the term, "Peak Experience".

Wikipedia's Encyclopedia states:

"A peak experience is a moment accompanied by a euphoric mental state often achieved by self-actualizing individuals. The concept was originally developed by Abraham Maslow in 1964, who describes peak experiences as "rare, exciting, oceanic, deeply moving, exhilarating, elevating experiences that generate an advanced form of perceiving reality, and are even mystic and magical in their effect. There are several unique characteristics of a peak experience, but each element is perceived together in a holistic manner that creates the moment of reaching one's full potential."

Maslow's Hierarchy of Needs placed self-actualization—reaching one's full potential—at the top of the pyramid of life. He considered the peak experience to be one of the paramount goals of life, as it is an indication of self-actualization.

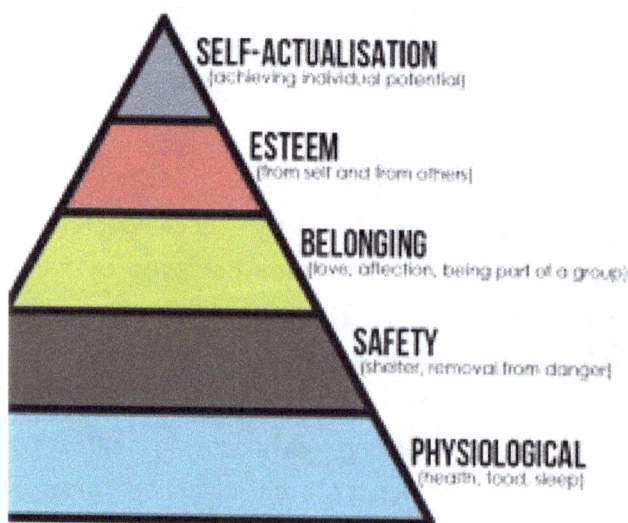

My own Peak Experience leaped over a couple of the above stages, and culminated in a profound prophetic vision of creating an international humanitarian project.

The vision calls upon the nations of the world to help in rescuing refugees and migrants. But to where, and where better than in a vast, modern and diverse land of mountains, lakes and prairies as in Canada, for example, with a relatively low population, capable of absorbing its fair share of the less fortunate inhabitants from countries with different cultures.

Is Canada the best match to ignite the vision on a path for aiding migrants and refugees? My research confirms that Canada qualifies to be a strong leader among leading countries that welcomes the down trodden, and it also has the advantage of being a truly multicultural nation. This is Canada's foremost identity.

But before considering this humanitarian project, it is important to understand the source of its inspiration. Maslow's findings identify that a Peak Experience, by implication, is **a supernatural happening.** This is something I personally and readily concur with. So, let me get right into this something that is so rare and unusual. My peak experience was an extremely positive and liberating event, but it was so incredible that one may have received the opposite impression, especially if that evaluation was left to my wife, Arlene, to decide upon. Due to the hardships of my life, and consequently that of my wife's, she had her share of doubts, as we all are prone to have many times in life.

MY PEAK EXPERIENCE

This unique experience began a long time ago on a Friday evening in February of 1970 when I happened to go on a weekend retreat at Villa Maria, a Roman Catholic retreat house located just outside of Winnipeg in St. Norbert. I drove there in a half an hour, and arrived at a park-like setting dotted with evergreens. I left my car in the parking lot and walked towards the charming building embraced by a variety of trees. Upon entering, I received a warm greeting, and was shown to my room. More men arrived and before long we all gathered in the conference room. In this relaxed and very restful and beautiful environment, I gradually started to settle into a tranquil and low-key spiritual program.

By the next afternoon, Saturday, February 7th, 1970, I reached a state of complete peace and total well-being. Words will never describe what I experienced, but I was in my room, and I was just sitting back in an easy-chair and gazing out the window towards a tree very close-by. As I was doing so, I was relaxing more and more, but moving deeper and deeper into a realm of perfect peace.

Suddenly, it dawned on me that this was February 7th. I sort of knew that, but this was a special February 7th. And that's what pushed me over the top! It was five years later! It was an anniversary! It was five years ago from when I had a shattering breakdown. I suddenly realized that since then, I had gone through five of the most strenuous and demanding years of my life. In spite of all the intense and sustained pressures, I was still absolutely okay!

As it was, already I was in an inspiring, peaceful, restful, consoling and meditative space, but now on top of it, I became saturated with euphoria at that thought. I was delighted by the sudden discovery of the enduring stability of my mind, and I was grateful. The sheer realization and gladness catapulted and virtually boosted me into a higher and most blissful state of consciousness imaginable.

As I was gazing out the window, I became very aware of the tree that stood only a few feet away from me. Then I sensed a presence. a living presence. A sacred presence. It was as though the tree had a living soul, and a living personality. I could fully sense and perceive the presence of that soul. I also became aware of the clouds and the entire scene, and all of nature took on a very reverent quality. Everything was blended in harmony, and had a sacred, living personality and was emitting a vibration and a pulsing life energy that was silently communicating.

At a subliminal level what was also registering on my mind was the almost imperceptible mesh of the window screen. I wasn't consciously aware of that, but on reflection, it may have been the mesh screen that first suggested to my mind that behind all that I was seeing there was a base of unity holding everything together. The entire landscape in my visual field was united. There were separations, but there were also connections, and just as in all of life, there was an underlying unity. I was led to become keenly aware of that reality. And not only was there unity, but all the world was united, and I was uniting with it all. All—all—the entire—complete --perfect universe! I was transcending!

At that time, I didn't even know what that word meant, but I certainly found out what the experience meant. Everything! I'll say it again--

it meant no less than—everything! I was highly elated and filled with absolute ecstasy. I completely transcended into oneness, into unity, into bliss, and into a place of reverence and holiness. I arrived at the royal door of the sacred estate of the prince of peace, and was intimately experiencing the peace of God that passeth all, all, understanding.

I imagine that I was on this threshold for only a few minutes, and then, as I was gazing out into the distance through the boughs of the overhead trees, my eyes drifted to a broken limb that was just hanging there. In a moment or two a great apprehension came over me, almost a panic. I had an acute sense that someone at home was in trouble.

After a few moments, as quickly as it came, the feeling passed, and I drifted back into the awesomeness of bliss. This was truly an "overcoming" experience. I was now above all the problems of the world, and apparently in a state of unitive consciousness. From this spiritual perspective, there were no real problems to earthly existence, none whatsoever, but an entire and perfect sense of well-being.

Since that experience I have never had any concerns about my mental stability. That completely cleared the air for me. I could breathe easy. This was a totally liberating event that healed me of all fear.

SHATTERED

But there was one problem. I made the mistake of coming down from this mountaintop experience by returning straight home after the retreat—before I was irreversibly established in this blissful state. But I noticed that there were no problems while driving home through all the traffic. I noticed that in no way did that distract me from the sublime peace, and calm, and utter contentment that I was feeling.

When I arrived home, however, my wife couldn't understand what happened to me. Arlene was a couple of months pregnant with our fourth child at that time, and maybe she was either too sensitive, or not sensitive enough. She thought that I was weird when I was just so calm and detached. I guess she was afraid that I might be going "wingy." Consequently, she agitated and agitated and wouldn't stop until she shook me out of this frame of mind by bringing me to a point of anger, and completely putting down what

I was feeling. This sublime and delicate space was shattered like the bursting of the most beautiful bubble one could possibly imagine. I felt robbed of truly the most beautiful experience of my entire life. Something very, very sacred had been broken.

THE BROKEN LIMB

That was not all that was broken. After my arrival at home, I soon learned that one of the neighbours, who lived right next door, at Dorothy and Harold Leonhardt's place, had fallen and broken an arm on the weekend. Apparently, this happened at the same time that I was focusing on that broken tree limb at Villa Maria, and became gripped with strong apprehension. In addition to having had an extremely exotic episode, I also had a foreboding and psychic experience.

SPIRITUAL EVALUATIONS

Again, I can use a phrase to describe this ecstatic episode of peace as I used in regards to an earlier revelation experience. Again, I can say: "never before or never since have I ever experienced anything like that." Comparing the two, if that were possible, they were both very impressive, but somewhat different.

The first was more of a directing, exciting, energizing, convincing, motivating and empowering experience. The latter was more of an inspiring, beautiful, contenting, reassuring, profound and supremely blissful experience. Both had a prophetic quality.

The event at Villa Maria was an ultimate spiritual happening, and I know that it really cannot be imagined. It has to be experienced. But I also know that it is a very rare, elusive, and absolutely the most precious experience anyone could ever want to have. As a result, from time to time, naturally I tried to capture it again. Although it is very elusive, that is not impossible. I have since had a few minor transcendental episodes, but none have ever come anywhere near to that ultimate magnitude.

Over the ensuing passages of time, however, my life would not be at all peaceful due to the sharp turn of events relentlessly amassing just around the corner. Nonetheless, I have had a chance over the years to make a few investigations of transcendental, peak experiences, and altered states of consciousness. I have been interested in exploring only the natural and genuine variety, totally avoiding the pitfalls of all drug-induced states that I felt would be artificial and not actually real.

I also have made a study of the reality of the phenomena from the standpoint of the psychology of religion, and have taken a course on this subject in Canada at the University of Manitoba. I know enough about the subject now to know that these types of experiences, although relatively rare, are nevertheless common to people the world over. Generally, they fall into two descriptive categories: the theistic and non-theistic depending on one's cultural or religious background. Not only is the phenomenon respected as being very precious or sacred, but also indeed it is the most ultimate experience that any human being could ever have.

A BIG DIFFERENCE

It was a pity that I lost something so precious on my arrival back home. Thinking that I might be going off the deep-end, I guess my wife thought that she would be my saviour, but as my saviour, she has fallen very short. God! If that was crazy—let me have it with both barrels! The fact of the matter is that I happened to have been in a position to compare the difference. I had a hell of an experience five years earlier in February of 1965 when I suffered a breakdown after working on the Winnipeg Police Force. Since then, I lived with some fear that once I had an episode, I might be susceptible to having another. I held this fear for a very long time, particularly owing to the fact that a breakdown of the kind I underwent, resulted in a very mentally agonizing and tortuous time. But the experience in February of 1970 was the very opposite. This was a heavenly experience! I was probably as close as anyone ever could get to heaven on earth.

More was shattered, however, when in the fall of 1970 my wife lost our last baby at birth due to anencephaly. I guess I wasn't as sensitive as I might have been to my wife who experienced this loss in a very intimate way, and in a way that I couldn't possibly imagine after carrying a child to full term.

PART TWO

THE PROPHETIC VISION

Although my altered state of mind was shattered, nevertheless this peak experience left quite a residual effect. There was a little something salvaged from that superlative event. From it soon came the conception of the prophetic vision—kept safely sheltered and gestating over a number of years under the burgeoning name of the Pyramid of the West, or the Keystone of the West, as it may be called.

Under any title, however, the birth of the prophetic vision now can be revealed. Emerging before your eyes is a significant and challenging humanitarian endeavour in its initial form:

THE ORIGINAL CONCEPT

This rudimentary stage is expandable to accommodate the critical mass of Migrants and Refugees and others. It is a universal system, a concept designed for the participation of governments, private sectors and various religious denominations, and serving the needs of the international community at large.

The Pyramid of The West consists of an ecumenical retreat resort, an interfaith chapel, a conference centre for skills training and teaching, an international hotel or villa, an ethnic restaurant, and a health spa for the healing and fitness of body, mind and spirit.

Suggested for a location in Canada, the province of Manitoba may be ideal. The area of Birds' Hill Park is close to the geographical centre of North America, and the International Peace Gardens. Since Manitoba is the Keystone Province of Canada, this concept also may be known as Keystone Canada:

THE INTERNATIONAL VILLA

This venture may be seen as a contribution to local and international education and world development based generally on a Pestalozzi school of thought. It would incorporate a modified version of the United Kingdom's Pestalozzi Children's Village[2] in the physical range and under the spiritual concern of The

Pyramid of The West. This would result in a number of benefits to the entire complex, not the least of which would provide "a rudder" to assure that the wake of authentic ecumenical activity stays on an open and true course, and navigates amid the troubled waters of all peoples and nations.

The International Villa would also benefit as a tourist attraction, providing rooms with a range of exotic decors. Tourists could be offered a choice of staying in:

The Jordanian Room

The Nigerian Room

The Egyptian Room

Or, whatever national rooms that would be adapted under a Pestalozzi program. Tourists would have an opportunity to encounter an international setting. Those with vacation fever could wet their appetites by sampling international intrigue while others could quench their thirst by the crystal-clear waters flowing serenely from a spiritual oasis.

During the majority of the year, these national rooms would be available for resident students whose families have migrated from various countries who would then live in an atmosphere they would be accustomed to, that is, with peers and in rooms retaining their original cultural characteristics. This would be consistent with the Pestalozzi philosophy of preserving each student's national identity in an educational and humanitarian program. This overall concept provides a prestige opportunity to forward justice and peace in the world by forwarding international development, and meeting the dire needs of migrants and refugees including many Ukrainians:

Canada Receives Unlimited Number of Ukrainians Fleeing from War

(Credit: Canada Immigration)

MANITOBA'S MULTICULTURAL MOSAIC

In Canada in 1970, the City of Winnipeg celebrated Manitoba's Centennial. Its multicultural grandeur evolved from the Manitoba Mosaic made up of a diversity of languages and ethnic groups, composed of a multitude of volunteers and a large variety of festivals with ethnic foods and entertainment.

FOLKLORAMA

This gave rise to Folklorama, The Festival of The Nations, located in Winnipeg. Folklorama is the largest of its kind in the entire world. Currently, it has grown to 40 cultural pavilions featuring, for example, Africa, Argentina, Ethiopian, First Nations, Israel, United Kingdom, Chinese, Italian, Métis, Mexican, Philippine, Polish, Serbian, Ukraine and so on.

As well, there are others in the city and throughout Manitoba, such as: the Arborg Fair & Rodeo; Dauphin CountryFest; Festival du Voyageur; Misipawistik Oskatisak Pow Wow; St-

Pierre-Jolys Frog Follie; The Winnipeg Folk festival; Winnipeg International Children's Festival; and just too many more to mention.

At the same time, after my peak experience in 1970, the concept of The Pyramid of The West came to mind. I sensed that this was an enormous ecumenical opportunity for various groups to build unity through diversity as exemplified by the Manitoba Mosaic. This concept is a powerful vehicle capable of taking in and boarding many migrants and refugees, and fulfilling a humanitarian purpose.

Furthermore, I thought that due to the universal nature of this lofty ideal, it probably could only materialize through the participation and international influence of major religious groups, such as the vast Roman Catholic Church. And most likely with the co-operation of the Vatican, whose involvement I was keenly interested in. Finally, I also knew that this influential church would need a perfectly good reason to get behind such a major undertaking, but the prime motivation I had was still far from explainable and presentable.

After all, at that time, I was dealing with my own subjective mystical or spiritual experiences that in no way could I describe and objectify, or verify.

I was left only with faith. In physical terms-- how could I budge the Rock of Gibraltar? And besides the physical, in spiritual terms—how in the world could I move the ancient and massive Roman Catholic Church?

The ever-increasing crisis of migrants and refugees provides the answer. By expanding this original concept, the crucial needs of many displaced persons can be met. I now trust in the goodness of Canada, and the leadership of the Roman Catholic and other churches to ultimately accomplish this humanitarian goal. After all, they do subscribe to St. Matthew, 25:32—46:

"All the nations will be gathered, and he will separate them one from another, as a shepherd separates the sheep from the goats. He will set the sheep on his right hand, but the goats on the left. Then the king will tell those on his right hand, 'come, blessed of my father, inherit the kingdom prepared for you from the foundation of the world; for I was hungry, and you gave me food to eat. I was thirsty, and you gave me drink. I was a stranger, and you took me in. I was naked, and you clothed me. I was sick, and you visited me. I was in prison, and you came to me.'"

ADVANCE THIS CAUSE

To date, several preliminary steps have been taken to raise and advance this humanitarian project and to transform a simmering prophetic vision into a tangible reality. Initial information has been distributed to several influential Manitobans and Canadians and others.

Apart from the guidance of prominent leaders, and the hopeful involvement of philanthropists, the valuable participation of world citizens is encouraged to fully accomplish The Prophetic Vision.

This may be done, not only by ordering copies of this book, but also by extending my Canadian petition, formerly trialled on the Internet.

But the sudden onslaught of the Covid-19 Pandemic brought my petition, and a brief experiment on the Internet, to a screeching halt! However, to salvage the original design, I have preserved the elements in print, as follows:

A REFUGE FOR MIGRANTS AND REFUGEES

"NOW IS NOT THE TIME

TO LOOK AWAY FROM SUFFERING

BEYOND OUR OWN BORDERS."

"I was in prison

and you came to me."

A PETITION TO BUILD & PROMOTE:

A Humanitarian Project In Canada

as inspired by

The Prophetic Vision

to aid in overcoming a worldwide crisis

39

by creating

A Refuge For Migrants & Refugees

About The Book

This book explains and describes the project in some detail, but is not absolutely required for signing the petition. **It is the petition on behalf of the suffering migrants and refugees that may be more important**, and not necessarily the book. **People from other countries** also may sign their petition to support Canada in a combined **international effort** to meet this worldwide challenge.

As our global society and world economy recovers, a petition may be re-established and signed and shared for the building of

A Refuge For Migrants & Refugees.

Your support and participation in this meaningful cause is greatly appreciated. Thank you very much!

Related Comments

From A Canadian

Humanitarian Aid Worker:

"You may feel ... you have learned what it means to be truly isolated. That your space has shrunk, your movement restrained, your freedom taken from you. No doubt, the COVID-19 lock-down has affected your livelihood and future.

However, you also know that things will improve, eventually. Your government is providing continuous support. There is a reason to hope. None of these certainties are available to millions of displaced families quarantined away from home in dreary camps -and overwhelmed host communities around the world. For them, there is no end in sight."

-- Marwa Awad, humanitarian aid worker.

And From Pope Francis ...

"Migrations, more than ever before, will play a pivotal role in the future of our world."

-- Pope Francis

(End of the copy of my petition as briefly on the Internet)

This appeal is transferable to all countries by placing a petition on the Internet for world citizens to sign to encourage Canada's relief efforts. However, this book now serves the same purpose, so, tangible support for this cause can be made directly by purchasing this book.

His Eminence
Michael Cardinal Czerny

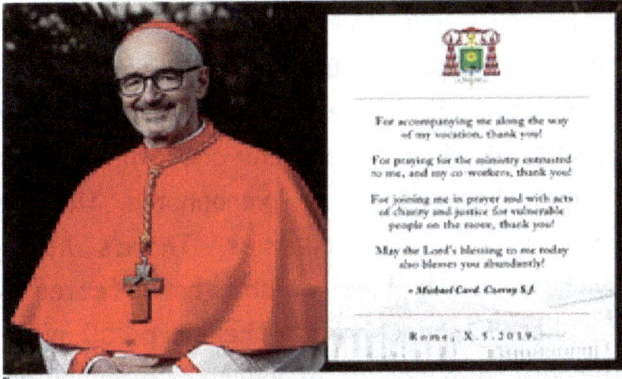

Pope Francis created a special section for migrants and refugees, he decided to lead it personally; and appointed Fr. Michael Czerny, S.J, and Fr. Fabio Baggio, C.S., to manage it starting in 2017. This small, action-oriented Vatican office helps worldwide to support those who endure forcible displacement due to conflict, natural disaster, persecution, or extreme poverty; it also supports victims of human trafficking.

Since 2017, Michael Cardinal Czerny has collaborated with His Holiness in all matters concerning the Section for Migrants and

Refugees in the Vatican's Dicastery for Promoting Integral Human Development. His Eminence emphasizes that this department, under the guidance of the Pope, has become one of the most important in engaging the urgent human phenomena of our times, the movement of people across the globe from war zones, poverty, economically depressed areas and ethnic zones, as well as addressing xenophobia that is spreading in many countries. There's hardly anywhere on the planet which is not affected by this phenomenon. Currently there are 250 million international migrants, of whom 22.5 million are refugees.

WHY SPONSOR A REFUGEE?

Consider the life of Michael Czerny whose commitment is to help men and women to live their lives and to live them to the full. His personal experience as a child refugee motivated his ministry. Born on July 18, 1946, in Brno, Czechoslovakia (in today's Czech Republic), he became **a child refugee at the age of 2** when his family had to flee from their homeland. Thanks to a personal sponsorship, they were able to settle in Canada. **What were the results of taking in this refugee?**

Father Czerny lived in Canada over 30 years. He entered the Society of Jesus in English Canada in 1963, and was ordained in 1973. He did graduate studies at the University of Chicago in an inter-disciplinary programme in humanities, social thought and theology and earned the doctorate in 1978. Dr. Czerny was the founding director of the Jesuit Centre for Social Faith and Justice, Toronto (1979 – 1989).

After the 1989 assassination of the Jesuits at the Central American University (UCA) in San Salvador, he became Director of its Human Rights

Institute (1990 – 1991) and Vice-Rector of the UCA (1991). For 11 years Michael served as Secretary for Social Justice at the Jesuit General Curia, Rome (1992 – 2002).

In 2002, he founded the African Jesuit Aids Network (AJAN), which assists Jesuits to respond to the HIV/AIDS pandemic; he directed AJAN for 8 years, and his exemplary service continues.

On October 5th, 2019, Pope Francis created Czerny a Cardinal. ***Canada can be justly proud of this newest Cardinal, Michael Czerny.***

There may be no better example of **"Why Sponsor A Refugee"** than this. It is an honour to work with migrants and refugees in the best way one can, and I urge my readers to kindly consider supporting this humanitarian effort as much as possible. Thank you.

MOTHER AND CHILD

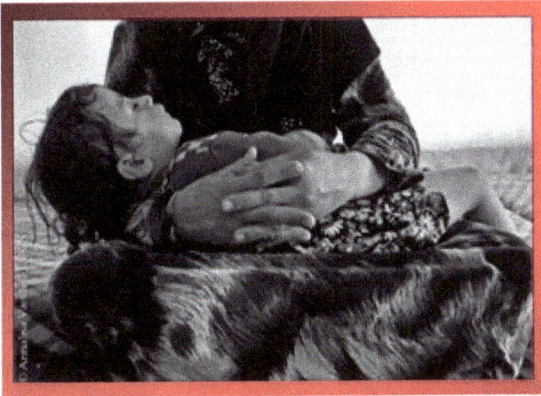

We ask that your crying will shake us from
our indifference; and open our eyes to those
who are suffering.

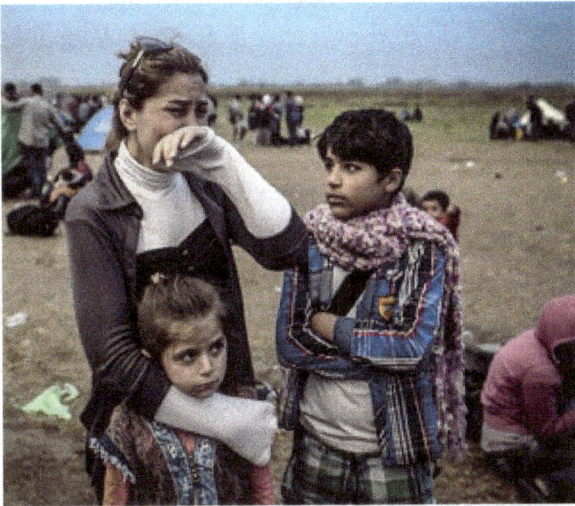

Refugees Won't Survive Without You!

PART THREE

In the face of the devastating world pandemic, apocalyptic climate change, torrential winds, catastrophic forest fires, raging floods, and a weakened world economy, the plans for THE PROPHETIC VISION naturally have been suspended. However, desperate times demand desperate measures! **What is the very best way** that may assure that Canada can continue to build this project?

Time brings new challenges, and many changes are in the wind that gravely impact Migrants & Refugees, and this also means that before too long, we can expect another **papal election.**

In preparation of the inevitable, and in seeking the absolute way to secure this humanitarian development, an open letter similar to this version, was delivered to the former Archbishop of Toronto, Cardinal Collins, and globally distributed to several other Cardinals. (An update may also be sent to them anew at an expectant time).

AN OPEN LETTER

TO THE CARDINALS

Dear Members of the College of Cardinals:

It is my special honour to address you collectively in respect to the eventual papal elections of the Roman Catholic Church, and I am seriously wondering:

WILL THERE EVER BE A POPE FROM CANADA?

I thoughtfully suggest that perhaps one may be found in the pages of my book, **"THE PROPHETIC VISION,** *A Peak Experience.***"**

Please note: This is not a future matter, but a current concern. You don't reap a future harvest without preparing the ground today. So, I suggest that it's timely to consider:

WOULD A CANADIAN BE A PRIME CANDIDATE FOR THE THRONE OF PETER, AND HOW COULD THIS HAPPEN?

Well, Canada and all the Cardinals from other countries are quite concerned about the worldwide crisis of migrants and refugees, acutely intensified by catastrophic climate change. As you know, this is one of the gravest and paramount issues of our times, and so dear to the heart of our Holy Father, Pope Francis.

As nature changes and accelerates, so must human activity adapt in its quest for salvation from existential threats. Our country along with others are dealing with the present and future consequences in lesser or greater degrees. I suggest that Canada has the greatest potential of all nations to develop an extensive program that can absorb multitudes of diverse migrants and refugees. Our country is already playing a significant role as a coveted refuge, but there is much room to do exceedingly more by speeding up the screening process, and designing and producing a controlled number of modern holding shelters.

I respectfully implore you, by this open letter, to encourage fellow-Cardinals and others throughout the Universal Church to support Canada in a bid to become a stalwart sanctuary for migrants and refugees. I'm sure they would be more than willing to press their efforts on behalf of so many suffering souls. The leaders of the Church that succeed in doing the most for the most needy fulfill the primary mandate of the Lord, Jesus.

With God willing, our country will continue to become a predominant homeland for migrants and refugees. This then places Canada on centre stage as a force to be reckoned with.

So, it is conceivable and appropriate that in an environment of such compelling spiritual need, a Canadian Cardinal, unsought as he may be, would become a strong and serious papal contender, fostering reconciliation and benefiting our First Nations and all sorts of Canadians.

But is Canada truly a hotbed for begetting such an honour? What has Canada to offer for being so notable? What creative project, plans or provisions are possible? In other words, what is there to recommend Canada that will garner the vital and expressed support of the Church and future Cardinal-Electors?

I cordially invite you, and all other Cardinals, to closely consider **"THE PROPHETIC VISION, *A Peak Experience.*"** Copies may be acquired by anyone wishing to contemplate this proposal, and may be available locally or internationally at Amazon or other Book Distributors.

Please prayerfully review The Prophetic Vision to discern the potential for substantially and ultimately alleviating this particular crisis.

However, as ambitious and as grandiose as this plan may seem, nevertheless, it will not resolve the overwhelming crisis of migrants and refugees, but I hope that at least this effort may help in a significant way to address this tremendous dilemma.

The success of the College of Cardinals in electing a Canadian pope provides **the best assurance** that this meaningful, international humanitarian project will continue to be developed.

I am grateful for all your prayers and efforts, and I humbly thank you on behalf of all Migrants & Refugees.

I am sincerely yours,

L. D. (Lorne) Glowicki

FURTHERMORE, I am most grateful to His Holiness, Pope Francis for journeying to Canada to meet with Indigenous communities, and personally express his heartfelt apology for Catholic involvement in residential schools.

(Credit L'Obsservatore Romano)

The arduous pilgrimage of Pope Francis attests to his complete willingness to reconcile with all Indigenous people. His Holiness deeply regrets the sufferings caused by the Church, and adjures all Catholics to bring the wounds of the past into the healing of the present as well as into the future.

I am also especially grateful to His Holiness for the theme that was chosen for the 2023 **World Day of Migrants and Refugees**. It is an emphatic and wise acknowledgement that creative ways must be found to reduce the outflow and heartbreak of prospective migrants and refugees by supportive ways to assure their human rights to remain in their own homelands.

As just mentioned, as ambitious and as grandiose as a Canadian plan may seem, nevertheless, it will not resolve the overwhelming crisis of migrants and refugees all by itself. New and innovative ways must continuously be found as put forth in the following message by the Holy Father:

MESSAGE OF HIS HOLINESS

MESSAGE OF HIS HOLINESS, POPE FRANCIS FOR THE WORLD DAY OF MIGRANTS AND REFUGEES

Dear brothers and sisters!

The migratory flows of our times are the expression of a complex and varied phenomenon that, to be properly understood, requires a careful analysis of every aspect of its different stages, from departure to arrival, including the possibility of return. As a contribution to this effort, I have chosen to devote the Message for the 109th World Day of Migrants and Refugees to the freedom that should always mark the decision to leave one's native land.

"Free to leave, free to stay" was the title of an initiative of solidarity promoted several years ago by the Italian Episcopal Conference as a concrete response to the challenges posed by contemporary migration movements. From attentive listening to the Particular Churches, I have come to see that ensuring that that freedom is a widely shared pastoral concern.

"An angel of the Lord appeared to Joseph in a dream and said: 'Get up, take the child and his mother, and flee to Egypt, and remain there until I tell you; for Herod is about to search for the child, to destroy him" (Mt 2:13). The flight of the Holy Family into Egypt was not the result of a free decision, nor were many of the migrations that marked the history of the people of Israel. The decision to migrate should always be free, yet in many cases, even in our day, it is not. Conflicts, natural disasters, or more simply the impossibility of living a dignified and prosperous life in one's native land is forcing millions of persons to leave. Already in 2003, Saint John Paul II stated that "as regards migrants and refugees, building conditions of peace means in practice being seriously committed to safeguarding first of all the right not to emigrate, that is, the right to live in peace and dignity in one's own country" (Message for the 90th World Day of Migrants and Refugees).

"They took their livestock and the goods that they had acquired in the land of Canaan, and they came into Egypt, Jacob and all his offspring with him" (Gen 46:6). A grave famine forced Jacob and his entire family to seek refuge in Egypt, where his son Joseph ensured their survival.

Persecutions, wars, atmospheric phenomena and dire poverty are among the most visible causes of forced migrations today. Migrants flee because of poverty, fear or desperation.

Eliminating these causes and thus putting an end to forced migration calls for shared commitment on the part of all, in accordance with the responsibilities of each. This commitment begins with asking what we can do, but also what we need to stop doing. We need to make every effort to halt the arms race, economic colonialism, the plundering of other people's resources and the devastation of our common home.

"All who believed were together and had all things in common; they would sell their possessions and goods and distribute the proceeds to all, as any had need" (Acts 2:44-45). The ideal of the first Christian community seems so distant from today's reality! To make migration a choice that is truly free, efforts must be made to ensure to everyone an equal share in the common good, respect for his or her fundamental rights, and access to an integral human development. Only in this way will we be able to offer to each person the possibility of a dignified and fulfilling life, whether individually or within families. Clearly, the principal responsibility falls to the countries of origin and their leaders, who are called to practice a good politics – one that is transparent, honest, farsighted and at the service of all, especially those most vulnerable. At the same time, they must be empowered to do this, without finding themselves robbed of their natural and human resources and without outside interference aimed at serving the interests of a few. Where circumstances make possible a decision either to migrate or to stay, there is a need to ensure that the decision be well informed and carefully considered, in order to avoid great numbers of men, women and children falling victim to perilous illusions or unscrupulous traffickers.

"In this year of jubilee you shall return, every one of you, to your property" (Lev 25:13). For the people of Israel, the celebration of the jubilee year represented an act of collective justice: "everyone was allowed to return to their original situation, with the cancellation of all debts, restoration of the land, and an opportunity once more to enjoy the freedom proper to the members of the People of God" (Catechesis, 10 February 2016). As we approach the Holy Year of 2025, we do well to remember this aspect of the jubilee celebrations. Joint efforts are needed by individual countries and the international community to ensure that all enjoy the right not to be forced to emigrate, in other words, the chance to live in peace and with dignity in one's own country. This right has yet to be codified, but it is one of fundamental importance, and its protection must be seen as a shared responsibility on the part of all States with respect to a common good that transcends national borders. Indeed, since the world's resources are not unlimited, the development of the economically poorer countries depends on the capacity for sharing that we can manage to generate among all countries. Until this right is guaranteed – and here we are speaking of a long process – many people will still have to emigrate in order to seek a better life.

"For I was hungry and you gave me food, I was thirsty and you gave me something to drink, I was a stranger and you welcomed me, I was naked and you gave me clothing, I was sick and you took care of me, I was in prison and you visited me" (Mt 25:35-36). These words are a constant admonition to see in the migrant not simply a brother or sister in difficulty, but Christ himself, who knocks at our door. Consequently, even as we work to ensure that in every case migration is the fruit of a free decision, we are called to show maximum respect for the dignity of each migrant; this entails accompanying and managing waves of migration as best we can, constructing bridges and not walls, expanding channels for a safe and regular migration. In whatever place we decide to build our future, in the country of our birth or elsewhere, the important thing is that there always be a community ready to welcome, protect, promote and integrate everyone, without distinctions and without excluding anyone.

The synodal path that we have undertaken as a Church leads us to see in those who are most vulnerable – among whom are many migrants and refugees – special companions on our way, to be loved and cared for as brothers and sisters. Only by walking together will we be able to go far and reach the common goal of our journey.

Rome, Saint John Lateran, 11 May 2023

FRANCIS

The above words are generally reflective of all future **World Day of Migrants and Refugees** for they are emblazoned in Heaven forever! There may be no need to update them yearly in any of my updates, but to remember them indelibly by this book.

THE BIG

QUESTION

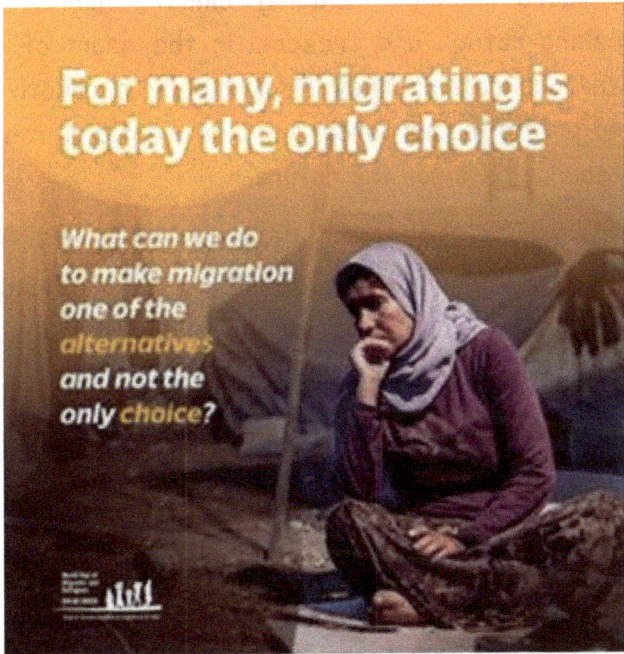

For many, migrating is today the only choice

What can we do to make migration one of the alternatives and not the only choice?

WILL YOU BE

PART OF

THE ANSWER?

IN CONCLUSION

Today, we still live in a war-torn world with many displaced people, including climate migrants, seeking refuge and freedom in the heart of a generous nation. They also embody a creative and potent labour force, and represent a vibrant resource base for the future.

They may be far from self-actualized, but with the encouragement of a caring and helping hand, they may rise to the top of a human being's potential—and live as one!

A WORD TO THE WISE:

Click VIDEO, available at:

https://migrants-refugees.va/resource-center/videos/

And scroll down to:

"It's a fundamental human desire

to live in freedom."

By

P. Agbonkhianmeghe Orobator

Seeking Refuge And Freedom

ORDER BOOKS

The Paperback Version of this book: https://www.amazon.ca/dp/1990742092 may be used for **FUNDRAISING** when purchased in volume at wholesale rates. Please contact eldeeglo@mymts.net to order. Thank you.

Otherwise, retail purchases, including E-books, may be ordered from local book distributors, or internationally from Amazon Books.

Please add your name in support of migrants and refugees and join the M&R mailing list by contacting https://migrants-refugees.va/

Thank you!

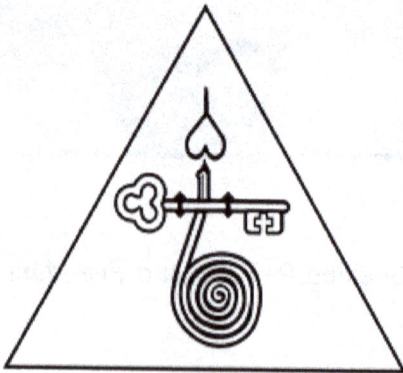

L. D. (LORNE) GLOWICKI

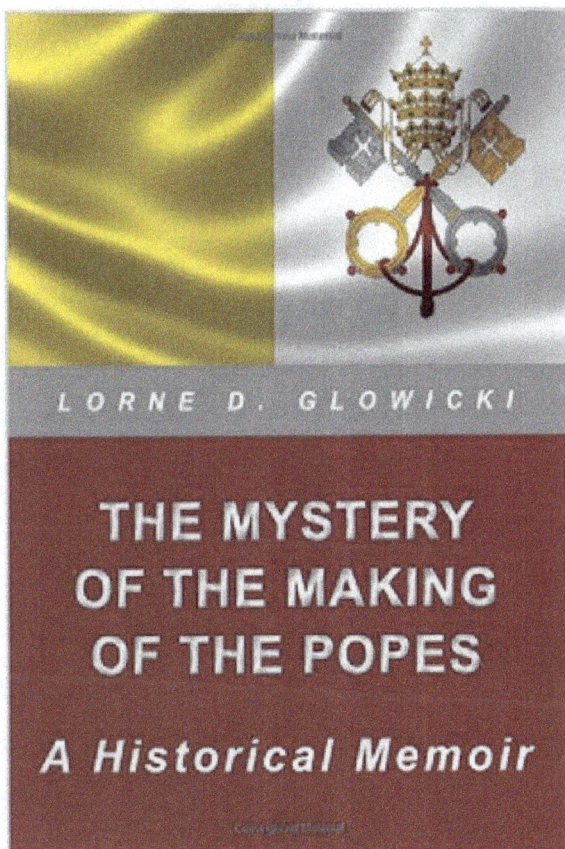

LORNE D. GLOWICKI

THE MYSTERY OF THE MAKING OF THE POPES

A Historical Memoir

A former police officer solves

a spiritual mystery and becomes

instrumental in papal elections

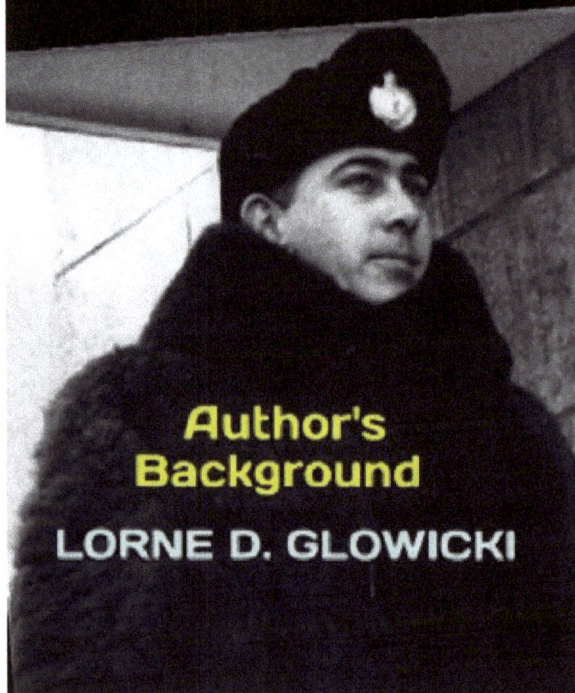

ROOKIE COP

Author's Background

LORNE D. GLOWICKI

Family Biography

and earlier Police Episodes not included in

The Mystery of The Making of The Popes

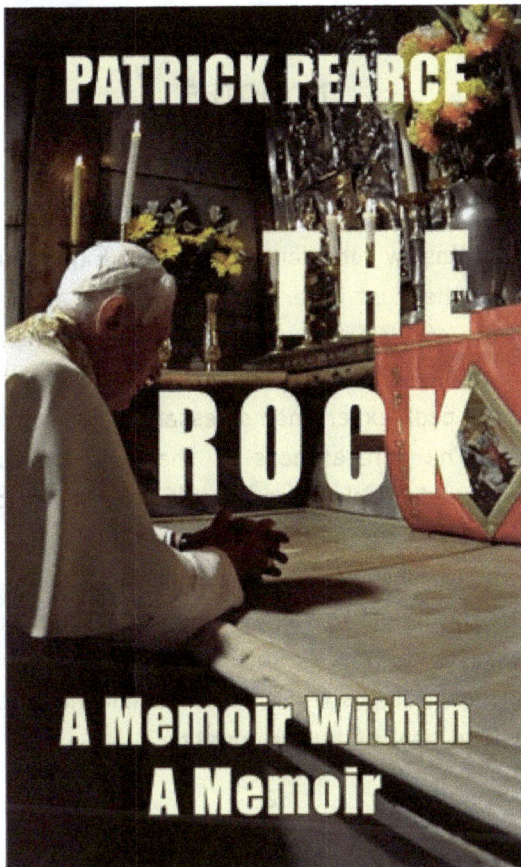

PATRICK PEARCE

THE ROCK

A Memoir Within A Memoir

Patrick Pearce is a pseudonym of my son who extrapolated excerpts from The Mystery of The Making of The Popes, and offers insightful comments from an inside perspective, and that also begins Patrick's own fantastic story!

ENDNOTES

1.

Abraham Maslow considered **The Peak Experience** to be one of the most important goals of life, as it is an indication of **self-actualization**. This moment of feeling wholly and completely is the true self and makes the peak experience an essential component of identity. The aftereffects of the peak experience leaves the individual to see himself and the world in a new way. He views himself more positively, he views life as worthwhile and meaningful, and most importantly, he seeks to repeat the experience. The peak experience is an exhibition of Maslow's emphasis on the quest for positive growth maximizing potential as **the true goal of human existence.**

2.

Finally, I've included some of my much earlier research that may be draw on in respect of the **Pestalozzi Children's Village**. This does not entirely apply to the proposed International Villa in Canada. But it provides a general idea that may be drawn upon, adapted, and specifically modified to enable the progressive and dynamic future of The Pyramid of The West.

HELPING THE WORLD'S CHILDREN

TO HELP THE WORLD

The countries of the western world have since the Second World War contributed in no small measure to the development of the emergent nations by making considerable grants of overseas aid, both financial and in kind. Such "significant aid" has made progress possible in many spheres of the economic life of the countries helped in this way. For the future of these nations and the training of their young people the need for education stands paramount amongst the priorities of their developing requirements.

In the field of human relationships the role of the voluntary society is still of great significance. It is in the field of humanities where aid is needed in no small measure. In all the developing nations there is an urgent need for secondary and further education, a need taken for granted by the western world but provided only at tremendous cost in the developing countries.

Many thousands of children whose abilities are demonstrated during their primary education as being fit for further courses are deprived of this opportunity through the sheer economics of their countries of origin. It is in this field that the Pestalozzi Children's Village Trust was the logical development of the British Pestalozzi Association, which was formed in 1947 to support the British House at the original Pestalozzi Village at Trogen in Switzerland.

When the Village first opened at Sedlescombe it provided training and education for children from the displaced persons camps of Europe and some 60 children passed through the Village between 1959 and 1963. All have now gone on to university, or technical education and training or have taken their place in the world. Fortunately the problem of refugees and displaced persons in Europe has been largely abated, and in 1964 the Pestalozzi Children's Village Trust decided to open its doors simply to those children who were deprived of the educational chances, which their abilities merited.

These children, now becoming young people, are the first, it is hoped, of a long line of youngsters who, selected because of their ability, will, when they return to their countries of origin, play a significant part in the development of their nations. Having acquired at the Pestalozzi Village not only academic education, for which they are indeed fitted, but an international attitude and a regard for tolerance and world peace-a background probably unique in this world today, they are potential leaders of their communities.

In each of the countries whence children presently come, the Trust has committees whose responsibilities begin with the selection of the initial group of children, under a set of strict criteria laid down by the Trust, and continue with the replacement as children leave the Village. These committees also select the national house-parents who come to Sedlescombe to live with and control the groups in which the children live. The committee's responsibilities will continue when the youngsters return to their countries of origin to ensure that they have the right job and are able to play the part for which they have been trained.

The criteria of selection include not only academic ability but also psychological suitability of separation from their parents for periods of five and eight years. The Council of the Trust hopes that at least once during their stay in the Village, the children will pay a visit to their homeland. This was made possible during the past summer by the generosity of subscribers and well-wishers who contributed to the travel fund. This allowed those who had taken "o" levels to visit their parents and, at the same time, study conditions in their homeland. These visits will play a significant part in the children's choice of career, enabling them to pursue those courses and studies for occupations most needed and most helpful in the development of their respective countries.

The Trust's work does not represent an immigrant operation in Britain. By living in national groups, maintaining their national language, their cultures and their religions, the youngsters will return not as strangers to their countries, westernised by five or eight years in the U.K., but as true nationals with the avowed intent of serving their communities and their countries.

At Sedlescombe today are groups of Thais, Indians, Nigerians, Jordanians and Tibetans, a total of 96 divided into seven houses, living together and working in an international community atmosphere and learning to appreciate the cultures of other nations and the difficulties with which other peoples are faced.

Educated at the local secondary modern, comprehensive and grammar schools, the children, because of the selection techniques employed, fully demonstrate their worthiness for secondary and further education. Trained by the Village in such crafts and skills as farming, carpentry, building, electrical engineering, farm machinery maintenance and many other disciplines, they learn to work for international community development.

This is being currently demonstrated by the appearance of a new house rising in the Village at Sedlescombe, built entirely by the skills of the youngsters themselves. Not only does this work give them the opportunity of learning the meaning of community development, but also working together as mixed nationalities they will take away with them, when they leave the Village, a feeling of **the brotherhood of man irrespective of race, colour or creed.**

And to my cherished readers:

I wish you every grace in the name of
God The Father, and The Son, and
The Holy Spirit.

www.ingramcontent.com/pod-product-compliance
Lightning Source LLC
Chambersburg PA
CBHW071341290326
41933CB00040B/1970